Tell ME What YOU Remember

SCHOOL

Sarah Ridley

W
FRANKLIN WATTS
LONDON · SYDNEY

Franklin Watts
First published in Great Britain in 2015 by
The Watts Publishing Group

Copyright © The Watts Publishing Group 2015

Series editor: Sarah Peutrill
Series design: Basement68

The Author and Publisher would
like to thank everyone who has
kindly contributed their photos
and memories to this book.

Dewey classification: 371'.00941'0904
HB ISBN: 978 1 4451 4009 4
Library Ebook ISBN: 978 1 4451 4010 0

Printed in China

Franklin Watts
An imprint of
Hachette Children's Group
Part of The Watts Publishing Group
Carmelite House
50 Victoria Embankment
London EC4Y 0DZ

An Hachette UK Company
www.hachette.co.uk

www.franklinwatts.co.uk

FSC
www.fsc.org

MIX
Paper from
responsible sources
FSC® C104740

Grateful thanks to St John's Green
Primary School, Colchester.

Picture credits: Peter Aves/
Franklin Watts. 3, 4. S B Davie/
Mary Evans PL: 17t. John Gay/
English Heritage NMR: 7t.
Henry Grant/Mary Evans PL:
5t, 11t, 13t, 15. Henry Grant/
Museum of London: 14, 17b, 19t.
The Sally & Richard Greenhill PL:
front cover t, 11b, 13b. Imperial
War Museums: 6. MOI/
Imperial War Museums: 8b, 9t.
Christine Osborne/Alamy: 3, 7b.
Popperfoto/Getty Images: front
cover c, 8c, 16, 21t, 23t. All other
photographs are kindly given
by the people who contributed
their memories.

Contents

Your School

When was your school built? In 1870, during the reign of Queen Victoria, the government decided that all children must go to school. Many schools in use today were built at that time.

Children at this school spend some of their school years in the old school and some in the new school.

The old part of St John's Green Primary School was opened in 1898.

The new part of St John's Green Primary School was opened in 2014.

Memories are what we remember about the past. Everyone has different memories about their schooldays. Talking to people about what they remember can help us to learn about the past.

David, born 1955, remembers...

My favourite lesson was PE. The gym equipment swung out from the walls of our school hall.

Funda, born 1968, remembers...

I loved my primary school. Pupils did not have to wear uniforms but I couldn't wait to wear mine!

Pre-school

From the 1930s to the 1960s, some children went to nursery school but most stayed at home until they were five. Gradually more nursery schools and playgroups opened, especially during the 1970s. All provided a place to play, paint pictures and sing songs.

These girls were washing dolls' clothes at their nursery school when the photo was taken in 1944. Find the wooden tub, the mangle for wringing out the clothes and the clothes horse for drying them.

Suzanne, born 1966, remembers...

I went to playgroup in my village. Like these children, I enjoyed playing with toys, as well as painting pictures at an easel and singing songs.

During the 1980s and 1990s, more mothers took on work outside the home. Some children went to day nurseries, like this one photographed in 1985. Many more day nurseries were built during the early 2000s.

FIND OUT MORE

Ask your parents and grandparents whether they went to pre-school.

7

School During the War

During the Second World War, school life was often difficult. Some teachers left to join the army, navy or air force. Books and paper were hard to buy. In some cities where air raids were expected, all the teachers and pupils were evacuated to the countryside.

Teachers took charge of their pupils during the evacuation of school pupils in September 1939. These children walked from their London school to catch a train to the countryside.

Most evacuees lived with local families. For city children, nature walks were a new experience.

Dorothy, born 1930, remembers...

1939–1945 Second World War.
By the end of 1939, a million children had left their homes in big cities and become evacuees in safer areas.

Our school took over a village hall (like the one in the photo) when we were evacuated. We were short of paper and pencils. The teachers cut the exercise books in half and we had half each. They did the same with the pencils.

FIND OUT MORE

Evacuees were given a list of clothes to bring with them. Look at the photo on page 8 to find the shoe bags, pillowcases and parcels used to carry their belongings.

Classrooms

Back in the 1930s and 1940s, most children sat at wooden desks, set out in long rows. Gradually schools replaced desks with low tables and matching chairs. Teachers wrote on blackboards using chalk, and then on whiteboards from the 1990s onwards.

Susan

Susan, born 1945, remembers...

We sat at wooden desks. The lids lifted up and we stored our exercise books and pencil cases inside. Some of us were going to Brownies after school so we had already changed into our uniforms.

Sarah, born 1963, remembers...

My classroom looked like this one, with desks pushed together. Once a week a TV was wheeled into the class on a trolley so that we could watch a BBC schools' programme.

Tom, born 1987, remembers...

Our teacher pinned our work to the classroom walls, as this teacher has. It was a big treat to use the only computer in the school. We left the class one by one to use it.

FIND OUT MORE

Look for the pictures celebrating the 1953 coronation of Queen Elizabeth II in Susan's classroom.

Lessons

In the 1940s and 1950s, classes often had as many as 50 children. Teachers usually stood at the front and taught everyone together. During the 1960s and 1970s, many teachers tried out new ideas in the classroom and worked with children in groups.

Lionel, born 1943, remembers...

I learnt some poems that I can still remember. We did lots of sums and practised handwriting every day, but we also spent a lot of time playing sport. I'm waiting to bat in this game of rounders.

Annie, born 1949, remembers...

Like these boys, I wrote with a dip pen at school. Every few words I had to dip the pen in the inkwell in the corner of the desk.

FIND OUT MORE

Ask your parents, grandparents or other adults to tell you about their favourite lessons at school.

Tom, born 1987, remembers...

In maths we used plastic blocks to see the difference between one unit and ten, as these children are. I liked working my way through reading books until I had finished the whole set.

School Food

During the Second World War, the government decided that schools should provide a healthy hot meal for their pupils. School dinners had begun.

Nick, born 1937, remembers...

Wartime food rationing made school lunches pretty dreadful. A teacher used to stand over me as I struggled to eat boiled herring or rabbit stew!

Peter, born 1950, remembers...

The class milk monitor fetched the milk and put a straw through the lid of each bottle. The milk was warm in the summer and frozen in the winter. I hated it!

Pippa, born 1964, remembers...

Everyone ate the hot school dinner at my junior school. Most meals were meat and vegetables and a hot sponge pudding with custard. Food was served at the table and cleared away by an older pupil.

Osman, born 1994, remembers...

Half my class ate packed lunches and the rest of us had a hot school dinner. When I was in Year 5 my school tried to make our dinners healthier. They banned turkey twizzlers!

1944 Schools had to provide healthy school meals.
1946 Free milk for all schoolchildren.
1968 No more free milk for secondary schoolchildren.
1971 No more free milk for 7-to-11-year olds.
1980 Schools no longer had to provide school meals. No more free milk for 5-7-year olds.
2008 The government asked schools to make school lunches healthier.
2014/2015 Free school meals for children aged 4-7-years old began in England and Scotland.

Out to Play

Irene, born 1939, remembers...

Over time, children have played conkers and clapping games, football and running around games, skipping and pretend games, as well as many others. While some games have hardly changed in 100 years, others were made up much more recently.

We spent a lot of time doing handstands and ball skills against the wall. We also did a lot of skipping, sometimes using a huge rope and taking turns to jump in.

These boys in the 1950s are playing conkers. They made a hole in the conker and threaded a piece of string through it. One boy holds his conker still while the other tries to smash it with his own conker.

Funda, born 1968, remembers ...

This photo shows girls using a long rope to play a skipping game in 1969.

Playtimes were usually spent playing jacks or football (boys against girls), using skipping ropes or playing games like 'What's the time, Mr Wolf?' Later on we just walked around chatting.

Over the last 50 years, many more schools have added climbing frames and other equipment. Compare this 1970s playground to one in your school.

Jordan, born 1993, remembers...

All sorts of games went on in the playground. I mostly played tag or British bulldog. There were playground crazes including Pokémon cards and Beyblades.

FIND OUT MORE

Ask older people to tell you about their playtime games. Can they remember the rules?

17

Special Days

More than anything, people remember the special days from when they were young. At school this might be taking part in a play, a school trip, sports day, a special assembly, a concert or other celebration.
What will you remember about your school days?

Jessie, born 1940, remembers...

I played the violin at this concert. I wonder what we sounded like! It must have been summer because we are wearing summer dresses and sandals.

David, born 1955, remembers...

December was great at school. We spent our days practising for the nativity play and making paper lanterns and paper chains.

Funda, born 1968, remembers...

Our school held a country dancing festival for all the local schools. I took part in it every summer. Pupils at my school came from a mix of different backgrounds.

Ben, born 1993, remembers...

Sports day was exciting. The whole school was divided into four big teams. Each child tried to win points for their team.

Moving On

Nick

Between the 1940s and the 1970s, pupils in their last year at junior school sat 11+ tests that decided which school they went to next – grammar schools for some, secondary moderns for most of the rest. From the 1960s onwards, most secondary schools became comprehensive schools. Some children have always gone to private schools.

Nick, born 1937, remembers...

My parents paid for me to attend this prep school. The headmaster was very strict but we were a happy lot. I left at the age of 13 to go to boarding school.

Sylvia, born 1945, remembers...

My brother and sister passed their 11+ but I didn't. I felt like the family failure for a while. But I enjoyed the practical lessons like sewing and cooking.

These pupils were photographed hard at work at a secondary modern school in 1962. Unlike pupils at a grammar school, alongside English, maths and other lessons they learnt skills such as woodwork, cookery or metalwork.

Amy, born 1977, remembers...

I remember the first day at my local comprehensive school. It was the first time I'd ever had to wear a school uniform. All of us sat in the huge school hall while we were divided into form groups.

1947 The school leaving age was raised from 14 to 15.
1972 The school leaving age was raised to 16.
2015 In England, all young people had to remain in school or training until they were 18.

Punishments

What happens when someone is naughty at your school? In the past, teachers were allowed to hit pupils with a cane, a ruler or a slipper. Or they could make them write out lines, such as, 'I must not talk in class' 100 times. From 1986, teachers in state schools were no longer allowed to hit their pupils.

Roger, born 1940, remembers...

I was not good at spelling. One teacher made my life miserable by making me stand on a chair while I tried to spell certain words.

Simon, born 1963, remembers...

My headmaster had names for his three canes of different size: Daddy, Mummy and Baby! Pupils at my school were caned across the hand if they broke school rules.

Timeline

Use this timeline to see at a glance some of the information in this book.

1870 The government decided that all children between the ages of five and 13 must attend school. School became free for all in 1891.

1930s Some children attended nursery schools or day nurseries but there were not enough places for everyone.

1939–1945 Many day nurseries opened to look after the children of women who were busy doing war work. During the war many children left cities for the safety of the countryside, where they had to share school places with the local children.

1944 The government reorganised secondary school education into grammar schools, secondary moderns and technical schools. All schools had to provide a healthy hot meal for their pupils.

1947 School leaving age was raised from 14 to 15.

1957 The BBC started to broadcast TV programmes for schools.

1960–1970s Most secondary schools became comprehensives.

1970s More nursery schools and playgroups opened with government support.

1972 The school leaving age was raised from 15 to 16.

1980 Schools no longer had to provide hot meals.

1986 Teachers were no longer allowed to hit pupils in state schools.

1988 The National Curriculum was introduced into schools.

1990s onwards Whiteboards replaced blackboards in many schools.

2000s Many more day nurseries opened.

2008 The government asked schools to make school lunches healthier.

2014/2015 Scottish and English schools serve free hot meals to 4–7-year-olds.

2015 All young people had to be in school or training until they were 18.

FIND OUT MORE

This photo was taken in 2004 on Eliza's first day at school. Compare your memories of starting school with those of older people.

Glossary

Air raid An attack by aircraft.

Blackboard A large board, used by teachers to write on with chalk.

Cane A slim stick used to punish a child, by hitting their hands or their bottom.

Coronation The ceremony when a king or queen is crowned.

Eleven Plus (11+) An exam taken by 10- and 11-year-olds to work out who should go to the local grammar school.

Evacuee Children became evacuees during the war when they were moved – evacuated – from cities to the countryside to keep them safe from air raids.

Food rationing Between 1940 and 1953, people were only allowed to buy fixed amounts of some foods in order to share them out fairly.

Inkwell A small inkpot that fitted into a hole in a school desk.

Jacks A game where you throw a small ball in the air and try to pick up as many small objects as possible before catching the ball again.

Mangle A machine used to squeeze water out of wet clothes.

Milk monitor The child with the job of handing out small bottles of milk to the other schoolchildren.

Nativity play A play that tells the story of the birth of Jesus Christ.

PE This stands for Physical Education, lessons where pupils exercised and learnt how to play sport.

Private school Parents have to pay for their children to attend a private school.

Queen Victoria The queen of Britain from 1837 to 1901.

Second World War The world war that took place between 1939 and 1945.

Turkey twizzlers A high-fat meal made in a factory using many ingredients, including turkey and breadcrumbs.

Index